SO,
I MARRIED MY
SHADOW:
POETRY & REFLECTIONS

LVF

Title: So, I Married My Shadow
Subtitle: Poetry & Reflections
Author: LVF
Publisher: Ink & Shadow Press
Publication Date: July 2025
First Edition Paperback
ISBN: 979-8-9908212-1-7

Description: *So, I Married My Shadow: Poetry and Reflections* invites
readers on a profound journey through their inner world and closest
relationships. Blending memoir, poetry, and reflective essays, this
collection explores intimacy, self-inquiry, and personal transformation.
At its core is a call to confront the "other" within—the shadow self—
where hidden fears, old wounds, and uncomfortable truths reside.
Revealed most vividly through our relationships, the shadow is not
something to avoid, but to integrate. Drawing from Jungian
psychoanalysis and esoteric wisdom, each piece lights the path from
unconscious patterns to conscious self-acceptance.

Keywords: self-help, self-reflection, self-acceptance, self-inquiry, self-
discovery, introspective, inspiration, healing, self-growth, forgiveness,
marriage, relationships, heartbreak, love & loss, grief, poetry, love
poems, esotericism, mysticism, occult, metaphysics, esoteric,
psychoanalysis, shadow work, Carl Jung, psychology, psyche, prose,
literature, memoir, mixed genre, women authors
Published in the United States of America

Visit us at LVFLVX.com

To my Other,
I don't know who I'd be
without you.

Disclaimer

This is a creative work and it is not a substitute for professional advice, diagnosis, or therapy. The author makes no guarantees about the accuracy or completeness of the content and assumes no liability for outcomes related to its use. Any resemblance to actual persons, living or dead, is purely coincidental. Events and details may have been changed or fictionalized to protect privacy.

Contents

PROLOGUE

I honestly had no idea what I was getting into when I decided to organize and publish my first poetry collection, *Tapes in Drag: Poetry & Remorse* last year, but I did know a few things. First, these poems meant something deeply personal to me when I wrote them over a decade ago. Second, I thought I had fully healed and moved on from those experiences, never expecting similar wounds to resurface in my marriage coinciding with my book's release.

This lack of awareness became a critical part of my growth. Without fully being aware, I embarked on a healing journey that would lead me into unfamiliar territory and ultimately bring me face-to-face with unprocessed emotions and experiences. This meant confronting unresolved issues, understanding my unmet needs, and exploring childhood traumas I unconsciously carried. The more I brushed these parts of myself aside, the more I realized there really was no escaping them.

Acknowledging and addressing these parts of ourselves and accepting them as integral—though painful pieces of who we are, is what initiates the healing process. To do so consciously and willingly is to *integrate the shadow.* It took me a decade to come full circle and finally understand the pattern for what it was.

As I walk you through this passage of self-reflection towards *wholeness,* it's important to understand the different aspects of our being. The *ego,* for example, is responsible for our decision-making, management of our morals, values and the conflicts we face when they are challenged by our social realities. It mediates between the individual's inner self and the external world, often shaping our sense of identity and self-esteem. It plays a critical role in balancing desires and reality, influencing how we perceive ourselves and interact with others.

In many spiritual and psychological traditions, the sun symbolizes the ego—the core of our individual identity and the sense of self we project onto the world. Just as the sun is the central force in our solar system, the ego drives our conscious actions, desires, and emotions, with these aspects orbiting around it like planets. The sun's light, radiating outward, reflects how the ego illuminates our sense of purpose and direction, guiding us through life's complexities.

Yet, just as the sun casts both light and shadow, the ego can also conceal parts of ourselves that we may struggle to see or accept. The ego is both necessary and demanding. It fuels our ambitions but can also blind us to our deeper needs and connections. When left unchecked, the ego can burn through relationships and distort our true essence.

Caught between the ego's need for validation and the soul's longing for wholeness, we exist in a state of duality, navigating the tension between our selfish desires and higher purpose. These inner conflicts bring to light our deficiencies and misalignments. The *id* is the most primal part of the psyche, driven by survival instincts and impulses, operating on the pleasure principle. It seeks immediate gratification of needs and wants, often disregarding social norms or consequences.

On the other hand, the *superego* represents the moral conscience and our inclination to uphold societal standards. It is developed through the internalization of cultural norms and parental guidance that acts as a counterbalance to the id, enforcing rules and ideals that guide behavior and promote ethical decision-making.

Interestingly, there is an aspect of our psyche that wasn't formally introduced until the early 20th century. Swiss Psychoanalyst, Carl Jung was the first to mention *the Shadow*, which he further elaborated in his book *Psychological Aspects of the Personality*. The shadow represents the unconscious aspects of the personality that an individual tends to reject or hide, often including fears, desires, and negative or unhealthy traits. It embodies the qualities and impulses that we deem unacceptable, leading to internal conflicts, but can also hold valuable insights and potential for personal growth when acknowledged.

Jung emphasized that unaddressed fears and unresolved shadow issues often surface as anxiety, self-sabotage, or conflicts with others. He warned that avoiding this inner work leads to projecting these hidden parts onto the world—shaping our reality in ways we may not realize. For this reason, I stress the importance of facing our fears directly instead of running from them. Whether we're aware of them or not, these anxieties tend to emerge in our lives uninvited. That's why it's essential to develop the tools and awareness needed to navigate them when they arise.

The ego, in its desire to maintain a certain image, rejects or suppresses parts of our personality that don't align with this ideal. These disowned traits, however, whether emotions, desires, or behaviors, don't simply vanish. Instead, they form the shadow self which lurks in the unconscious mind. The more the ego denies them, the stronger the shadow grows, leading to inner turmoil or outward behaviors we may not fully comprehend.

When this happens, our reactions and behaviors become shaped by fear rooted in the Qliphoth—a Hebrew term meaning *empty or corrupted shells*. These spheres represent a spectrum of shadow traits such as pride, deceit, cruelty, and arrogance. The Qliphoth are pathways of descent, embodying imbalance, chaos, and separation from Source. These traits signal that we're drifting away from wholeness. But we're not trapped by these ingrained patterns—recognizing them gives us the power to break free from hidden algorithms that confine us.

Sometimes, the darker sides of shadow emerge as *Machiavellian traits* that are expressed as manipulative, calculating, and self-serving behaviors, often driven by a focus on personal gain over ethical considerations. These traits include deceitfulness, exploitation of others, and strategic cunning, typically employed to achieve power or advantage in relationships and situations. Other shadowy traits like greed and envy vary in degree from person to person, influenced by upbringing, environment, and individual psychology.

While some may only brush against these tendencies in fleeting moments, others might grapple with more intense expressions of these traits, shaped by deeper wounds and unmet needs. Because of this, many of us fear revealing our vulnerabilities, imperfections, and insecurities. When we dread the unhealed parts of us and refuse to integrate, we build ourselves a prison. Recognizing that some individuals carry darker shadows than others allows us to approach this spectrum with nuance and self-awareness, acknowledging the shared humanity in our flaws while striving to transcend them.

Personally, I tended to mask and hide my struggles within my marriage and family for the sake of peace and appearances, not realizing how much it was affecting me emotionally, mentally, physically, and spiritually. Remaining in the dark, not just to the world, but to ourselves, ultimately hurts us the most.

As we each become more conscious of our flaws, it becomes easier to see them reflected in our relationships with others. Conversely, the less aware we are, the more we find ourselves at the mercy of our unconscious behaviors, ingrained survival instincts, and long-standing toxic patterns. It's often those we love most who become our greatest teachers, profoundly influencing our lives. They bring out our innermost joys and, paradoxically, reach into our deepest wounds.

Through this lens, I saw how my relationships, especially with my husband and parents—illuminated my vulnerabilities and areas in need of growth. Growing up, my parents were on their own journeys, learning as they went, much like everyone else. Too many parents lack the self-awareness required to adapt and embrace healthy parenting. I want to acknowledge how difficult parenting can be, particularly when true, healthy role models and mentors are scarce. Without these examples, it's all too easy to repeat the mistakes of our parents—who themselves often follow patterns passed down through generations.

The cycle of passing down unhealthy behaviors and patterns from one generation to the next is a core aspect of generational trauma. This cycle perpetuates not only the mistakes of the past but also the emotional and psychological wounds that accompany them. By recognizing and naming the struggle, we're creating the possibility of breaking the continuum, which often begins with self-awareness and a conscious effort to heal and adopt healthier practices.

Forgiveness, for example, is too often viewed as weakness rather than the pillar of strength that it is.

Without forgiveness, we become burdened by our suffering which inadvertently hurts us. However, forgiveness must be paired with healthy boundaries to truly liberate us from the patterns we've unconsciously forged.

Forgiveness is not only a release for the soul but a powerful force that can transform the course of our lives and break the cycle of generational trauma. In older generations, respect was often viewed as a privilege reserved for parents, with love frequently earned through obedience—especially in religious and military households. Authority and strictness were prioritized over empathy or understanding.

Today, however, we are witnessing a paradigm shift toward grace, compassion, and mutual respect. Conditioning children through fear and obedience can leave deep, lasting wounds that carry into adulthood. But by forgiving those who came before us—and embracing a new way of relating—we create the space to heal these wounds and nurture healthier generations.

Reflecting on the past, I recognize how crucial it is for a child to be accepted and loved for their authentic self, rather than being conditioned to earn affection through obedience and never taught to honor their personal boundaries. When these fundamental needs are neglected, we begin to carry a skewed sense of worth—where love feels conditional on compliance instead of grounded in mutual respect.

This sets the stage for a pattern in adulthood, where we overlook red flags in relationships and excuse unhealthy behaviors in the name of love. It's in this space that trauma bonds are formed—attachments based not on healthy connection— but on the need to prove ourselves worthy of love, even at the cost of our own well-being.

It's hardly surprising that many couples unknowingly replay patterns from their parents' relationships, often reliving old traumas and ingrained limiting beliefs. Although my parents divorced when I was very young, I still developed an idea of what love looked like— not from real-life examples, but from sitcoms that emphasized mutual respect, communication, and active listening.

Ironically, these were qualities I rarely experienced firsthand, which made expressing my needs, communicating openly, and asking for support a struggle well into adulthood. As a child, I wrestled with cognitive dissonance—knowing what my relationship with my parents could have been like if understanding and open communication had existed, yet being punished for trying to express myself.

The more I felt this rejection from my parents, the more I internalized a belief that I was unworthy of love. Subconsciously, I was setting myself up to experience just that. Some experiences leave wounds so deep that they change us at our core, and once they do, we're faced with a choice:

How has this pain influenced the way I see myself and relate to others?

What patterns am I unconsciously repeating because of this wound?

Choosing to grow and transform in a positive way is undeniably the more challenging path. It's a conscious decision that requires enduring discomfort and obstacles for growth. Therefore, we must ask ourselves: what does it truly mean to *better ourselves?*

Without a well-defined sense of what's healthy and grounded, we risk following a vague or misguided path. I know this because I once stumbled down that road myself, not yet understanding what wellness looked like. It is through my own mistakes and the lessons I've learned that I share this with you today.

That's why I believe that meeting my husband was no accident. We are complete opposites, each bringing strengths and perspectives that the other lacks. Our differences challenge each other in ways that push me to confront my shadows, as we inadvertently magnify each other's insecurities and expose our deficits.

Relationships become especially difficult when personalities, views, and values clash. Without grace or the ability to hold space, the chances for escalation increase. Similarly, the more you resist your shadow, the larger and darker it becomes— shaping the world around you until you're forced to face it and integrate it.

The caveat, then, is to stay aware of the transaction and give grace, recognizing that both parties are navigating their own complexities, and that healing is a process, not an immediate exchange. Every married couple, every long-term partnership, and those moving out of the honeymoon phase face struggles. Disagreements and conflicts are common, yet society often pressures us to keep up appearances, hiding the pain or neglect we may feel.

Idealizing our partner and expecting perfection also leads us to suppress our true selves, blocking meaningful growth. When we avoid honesty and vulnerability, our shadows grow stronger. These challenges in a relationship aren't signs of failure; they only become obstacles when we run away or dent them altogether. It's by embracing imperfections—both in ourselves and our partners—that real growth can happen.

Too often, long-term partners drift—pulled by restlessness, unmet needs, or the illusion that something better awaits. They seek fulfillment outside instead of confronting unresolved issues within. Some are tempted to leave, convinced someone else will treat them better. Maybe that's true—but without addressing our inner issues, we risk repeating the same patterns.

Avoiding difficult conversations and vulnerability means missing the emotional and spiritual growth a partner offers. Growth is always a choice—whether we stay or leave. The key lies in discernment. Running away keeps us trapped in old patterns; walking away, when done consciously, can open the door to acceptance and genuine transformation. Ultimately, facing these challenges head-on can lead to growth, but it does take two willing participants in a relationship to do that.

In my marriage, the real challenge wasn't our differences but rather his lack of awareness and my own denial. As Carl Jung famously said, *"Until you make the unconscious conscious, it will direct your life, and you will call it fate."* Jung emphasized the importance of shedding light on the unconscious as a path to emotional growth and healing. He believed that by uncovering hidden thoughts, emotions, and patterns, we gain insight into our true selves, moving toward a sense of wholeness—a journey he called *individuation*. Individuation is the process of becoming one's true self by integrating the conscious and unconscious aspects of the psyche, leading to personal wholeness and self-realization.

Without self-awareness, we're unable to tend to the wounded parts of ourselves that long to be seen, heard, and healed. In relationships, when a partner lacks this inner awareness, even simple conversations—about unmet needs, feedback, or boundaries—can quickly spiral into defensiveness and resistance, leaving little room for mutual growth.

This lack of self-awareness doesn't just affect how we relate to others—it also shapes how we respond to the emotions we've long suppressed. Repressed emotions don't disappear; they return as triggers. And in those moments, how often do we surrender to our survival instincts—fight, flight, freeze, or fawn? Our conditioned habits push us to repeat toxic cycles, while our often-buried free will quietly offers another way forward.

To engage that free will is to interrupt those patterns and forge new, healthier ones. It is the act of rewiring the brain—creating new neural pathways. These pathways are networks of neurons that transmit signals between different areas of the brain and body. They are the infrastructure for how we process information, respond to life, and form habits, memories, and behaviors.

By delving into our memories and cultivating the right awareness, we unlock the blueprint for constructing healthier pathways and, consequently, a brighter future. The journey towards self-acceptance and self-realization is both challenging and enlightening, revealing layers of unconscious patterns and deeply seated fears. With each revelation, we bring ourselves closer to forging a path towards healing.

While marriage isn't a requirement for this inner work, having a partner as a mirror can be a powerful catalyst. Marriage, at its best, is a psycho-spiritual journey—an intimate arena where we are invited to heal not only ourselves, but the generational wounds we've inherited and those we might otherwise pass on.

Lifelong partnerships offer a rare opportunity: to tend to the wounded adaptive child within us, to confront our fears, name our insecurities, and learn how to love each other through the pain. When we commit to this process, we open the door to lasting, transformative change.

So, I Married My Shadow speaks to the transformation possible in all relationships—not just romantic ones. Shadow work, the deep exploration of our hidden and suppressed parts, is a vital part of healing and self-discovery. But the truth is, many of us aren't fully prepared—emotionally, psychologically, or spiritually—to face ourselves at this depth.

Without the right support, diving into shadow work can feel overwhelming and even retraumatizing. That's why it's so important to approach this process gently, gradually, and with care—ideally with the guidance of a therapist, mentor, or supportive community.

This work isn't easy, but you don't have to do it alone. I'm here to walk with you—to help you meet the shadow, not with fear, but with the willingness to grow.

My goal with this book is to explore the many facets of the shadow self through poetry and reflection— inviting honest introspection as a path to both personal and relational growth. I've come to appreciate my shadow as the conduit through which I confront and begin to heal the wounded parts of myself. It is through this process—rooted in gratitude and grace—that emotional and spiritual restoration becomes possible.

When both individuals in a partnership are willing to face discomfort and grow together, deep healing and restoration are possible. But if you've done all you can and your partner continues to avoid the inner work, it may be time to seek support. A therapist or spiritual guide can help you discern your next steps and reconnect with your own path to healing.

I believe my audience will find resonance and validation in the pain expressed through these poems—written in a time of darkness, when I was still caught in the grip of inner bondage. Before freedom came, there was solitude. And in that solitude, I found solace. This collection is both a reflection of that journey and a testament to the healing that followed.

I wholeheartedly encourage my readers to embark on their own healing journeys, trusting that my words can serve as a steppingstone toward transformation. We hold the power to choose the version of ourselves we wish to become. By letting go of the parts that no longer serve us, we create the space needed to ignite that power and step into our fullest potential.

It is only through light that we can see and confront our shadows and find our inner strength to release them.

A Moment of Truth

Dear me,

If any of Shadow's actions hurt you— forgive yourself and detach from the ideas, thoughts, and limiting beliefs that cause resistance and therefore invite suffering. Don't feel betrayed, though I know it's hard not to. Remind yourself that through these experiences, I am finding both acceptance and liberation from the unhealed, unhealthy parts of myself. I am working tirelessly to heal and free you, for you have sought truth—and so you shall find it (Matt 7:7-8).

Remember, you hold power and authority over your Shadow, not the other way around. Hold this close the next time you feel unloved, rejected, unworthy, or abandoned...You're not those things. You are whole, capable, and loved (Rom. 8:38-39, Jer. 31:3, John 3:16).

CHAPTER ONE
IN THE DARK

The poems in this chapter explore the shadow side of relationships, raw vulnerability, and the pain of losing touch with who we are. They were written from a place where I had forgotten my strength and purpose, unable to see the deeper lessons within each struggle. Though there were times when I felt like a victim of circumstance, I realized that I am not. It's easy to feel powerless, especially when communication with loved ones feels futile and the weight of our challenges feels insurmountable, but, in truth, it is these challenges that are also the greatest catalysts for our growth.

These poems are not just stories about specific people or relationships. Instead, they offer glimpses into a shared human struggle. As you read, I invite you to imagine that the emotions expressed are your own. To release pain, we must first be willing to feel it. If any of these poems resonate with you, allow yourself to release it.

While the poems capture the intensity of these moments, the reflections in this chapter and the next provide ways to process these experiences with understanding, rather than judgment. Each reflection is paired with an introspective question, encouraging you to transform these difficult experiences into meaningful lessons that can enrich and empower your life and relationships.

I. charmed

i fell prey
to foolishness.
attracted to your delusions,
and
struck by your smile,
you showed me no mercy

Reflection:

Trust can sometimes cause us to overlook uncomfortable realities when we are swayed by what we *hope* is true rather than what is. It's not always the case, but when trust is extended too easily or indiscriminately, it can cloud judgment, blinding us of red flags and hindering our instincts. We may avoid confronting hard realities, holding onto an idealized version of things by having a deep desire for connection, approval, and belonging.

Trust is an active process requiring honest assessment, but *blind trust* skips discernment, assuming others are trustworthy without evidence. Though gullibility can be a vulnerability, it also reflects a hopeful belief in human goodness.

On the other hand, when exploited, it reveals the darker side of human behavior, often rooted in unresolved trust issues.

Recognizing these patterns in ourselves with compassion and nonjudgment allows us to uncover their root causes. Whether our trust issues stem from betrayal, trauma, or unmet needs, healing begins when we hold space for ourselves with intentional curiosity and grace.

Introspect:

How have past deceptions shaped how I trust now, and how might they be affecting my relationships?

II. martyr complex

peace is a facade
when you sympathize with the devil
and was raised to be a martyr

Reflection:

The quiet struggle of self-sacrifice is a deep inner conflict. When someone consistently makes excuses for poor behavior— whether their own or others, it often stems from a deeper pattern of self-neglect. This mindset can be especially prevalent in those who were raised to prioritize self-sacrifice over personal boundaries. We may rationalize mistreatment or justify poor behavior, believing it's our responsibility to endure or "fix" the situation at our own expense. This habitual dismissal of our own needs reinforces the idea that our worth is tied to our ability to give without limits or complaint.

Individuals raised in environments that idealize self-sacrifice may internalize the belief that asserting their needs is selfish or unloving. Breaking free from this cycle requires unlearning the conditioning that equates love with suffering, embracing self-worth, and recognizing that a healthy relationship honors boundaries and is founded on mutual respect.

Introspect:

Do I often find myself taking responsibility for others' actions or emotions, even when it's not mine to carry?

III. masking

denial hurts
because you simply don't want to know any better.
I simply don't want to know any better

Reflection:

Masking our true feelings often stems from a place of denial, where we shield ourselves from truths we're not ready to face. While this protective layer may provide temporary comfort, it ultimately prevents us from fully understanding our deepest needs and fears. Embracing the discomfort of self-discovery can be the first step toward genuine healing. By confronting these hidden truths, we allow ourselves to grow and move beyond our need to mask, opening the door to a more authentic and fulfilling life.

Introspect:

In what situations do I find myself masking my emotions, and what triggers this behavior?

IV. judgement

your strict punishment
frightens me.
yet, i've never felt so alone
in this world
without it

Reflection:

When others judge you harshly, especially without understanding the full context of your actions or struggles, it can create an internal dialogue of harsh self-criticism, leading to a sense of shame and isolation. This judgment may not only come from others but can also be internalized, manifesting as a relentless inner critic that undermines your confidence and peace. Over time, repeated exposure to such judgment can erode your sense of self, making you question your value and worth, often leaving you paralyzed in fear of further rejection or failure.

Be gentle with yourself when faced with perceived failures, losses, or shortcomings. Let self-compassion guide you, avoiding the traps of harsh self-judgment. Remember, we are all works-in-progress. By granting ourselves grace, we find the strength to learn, grow, and gently release the burdens of past mistakes and criticism we hold onto so tightly.

Introspect:

Do I internalize judgment from others, and if so, how does it affect my thoughts and actions?

V. discomfort

is it love if all you feel is comfort?
what is it then, when there's love but no comfort?

Reflection:

A lack of comfort in a relationship often creates a sense of emotional instability, leaving one or both partners feeling uncertain or unsupported. This lack of security can lead to frustration and distance, as both partners may become hesitant to fully invest in the relationship or meet each other's emotional needs.

On the other hand, too much comfort in a relationship can arise when both partners settle into a routine that prioritizes ease and familiarity. While comfort is essential for emotional security, an excess of it can lead to complacency. Over time, this lack of growth can stifle intimacy, leading to emotional stagnation and even resentment.

Comfort can also breed a fear of change, where one or both partners may resist stepping out of their comfort zone. The relationship, while stable, can begin to feel more like a habit than a dynamic partnership, losing the spark that originally drew you together.

Balancing nurturing support with constructive challenges enables us to step beyond our comfort zones and cultivate depth into your relationships.

Introspect:

How might an excess or limitation of comfort in my relationship be causing me to feel disconnected?

VI. disconnect

pleading,
always pleading
to be held
in your regard,
to be offered some comfort
or embraced in your bed sheets.
a soft, warm bed at your feet—
to forget
how cold it really is
between them

Reflection:

True vulnerability nurtures deep connection and intimacy starting within through honesty and trust. It creates a space for understanding and empathy to blossom, even with the risk of judgment or rejection. When vulnerability is absent, feelings of isolation can emerge, highlighting deeper longings to be nurtured. Supporting a partner who fears vulnerability calls for patience and gentle understanding. Offering support and celebrating their courage strengthens trust and deepens the bond. Even if progress is slow, remain patient and hopeful, knowing you're cultivating mutual growth and warmth together.

On the shadow side, facing rejection while being vulnerable can truly be painful, but it's important to remind yourself that rejection is not a reflection of your worth. Acknowledge the feelings of hurt without letting them define you and allow yourself time to process before responding or making decisions. Vulnerability, though risky, is essential for deeper connections and personal healing.

Introspect:

How do I respond when my vulnerability isn't matched, and what can I do to cultivate it in my marriage or relationship?

VII. complexes

i never wanted to feel small,
yet you led me there.
you needed something to hold on to,
something to make you feel whole.
each time you cut me down,
you grew larger,
putting me where
you wanted me to be —
beneath you

Reflection:

Superiority and inferiority complexes often stem from deep-seated insecurities and an imbalanced sense of self-worth. While a superiority complex may mask feelings of inadequacy through a façade of confidence, an inferiority complex internalizes those feelings, leading to self-doubt and constant comparison.

By acknowledging and exploring these insecurities, we can uncover how they shape our perceptions and behaviors, and how they often reinforce unhealthy patterns. Growth begins with cultivating self-awareness, recognizing the fears at the root of these tendencies, and practicing self-acceptance. Embracing your strengths while exploring your insecurities without judgment creates a healthy balance, fostering a more grounded and authentic sense of self-worth.

Introspect:

What past experiences or relationships might have shaped my tendencies toward either superiority or inferiority?

VIII. change

silently,
i grow distant—
not from who you are,
but from who i needed you to be.

Reflection:

The shift from closeness to distance in marriage or significant relationship often mirrors deeper changes happening within us—changes that can feel unsettling or hard to express. Recognizing this and fostering open, honest communication helps us stay connected to both our partner and our own evolving needs.

As we grow and heal, it's natural to hope for the same from our partner. However, each person's journey unfolds at its own pace, and growth cannot be rushed, nor can we force their transformation. Releasing the weight of expectations and letting go of the pressures we place on them allows us to focus on the present moment and appreciate others for who they are, easing division, and creating space for mutual understanding and growth.

Introspect:

How can I better communicate my evolving needs in my relationship? What are these needs?

IX. shame

i mistook survival for love
and silence for safety.

i kept quiet for years,
and am still afraid to say something

Reflection:

Hiding from shame often manifests guilt, especially when we avoid responsibility. Guilt serves as a signal that urges us to recognize our actions and make changes in our behavior that foster growth. Left unaddressed, it can deepen into shame, causing us to internalize blame, disconnect from our partner, and unconsciously self-sabotage.

Staying silent because of shame often stems from the belief that speaking out will lead to rejection, conflict, or judgment. Silence can initially feel like a safe refuge, a shield protecting us from shame or consequences. Yet, over time, it can shift from a form of protection to an emotional prison, weighing heavily on us. Unspoken shame also shapes the relationship without our knowing.

By finding the courage to express our truths, confront our fears, and embrace vulnerability, we can release ourselves from the weight of our shadow and begin the journey toward healing. Whether or not we confront our shame, the truth has a way of surfacing—making it all the more important to meet ourselves with compassion rather than adding to the weight we carry.

Introspect:

What fears and truths have I kept hidden, and how might they negatively be affecting me and my relationship?

X. dissociation

how does one go on
when your bones are broken
and your mind — separated from its body?

Reflection:

Trauma is not just the event that occurred; it's the lasting echo that reverberates within us, shaping our emotions, thoughts, and even the way our bodies react to the world around us. Its effects can linger long after the moment has passed, subtly influencing our relationships, decisions, and sense of self. One common response to trauma is dissociation, a protective mechanism that creates distance from overwhelming thoughts, emotions, and memories. While this shield may offer temporary relief, it often leaves us feeling disconnected—not only from our pain but also from our sense of wholeness.

This separation is a profound signal, inviting us to look within and confront the very parts of ourselves we've been avoiding. Healing from trauma requires more than survival; it calls for integration, a process of finding meaning in our pain and transmuting it into the larger story of who we are. By approaching our experiences with compassion and curiosity, we can transform even the deepest wounds into a source of strength and wisdom. This means that trauma isn't only defined by the pain or suffering it causes — it's also a *portal* to deep transformation *if* we're willing to face it rather than avoid it.

Introspect:

When I feel disconnected or dissociated, what triggers that response, and how do I cope with it?

XI. self-doubt/blind faith

how could you tell me
i never saw your potential?
i gave you my trust,
even when you broke it,
believing you'd rise

Reflection:

Self-doubt can distort both perception and memory, making it hard to discern whether we misjudged someone—or simply believed in them too much. We tell ourselves stories to keep hope alive, even when trust has been fractured.

It's painful to be accused of not believing in someone, when we know we silenced our own instincts just to keep believing. Sometimes the deepest betrayal isn't what they did, but how they reframed the past to suit their guilt. We begin to question not just them, but ourselves—our memory, our judgment, our worth.

But faith given freely is not a failure. It's a reflection of our capacity to love and to hope. The work is in learning when to stop giving it to someone who keeps asking for our trust with no intention of honoring it.

Introspect:

For the one who doubted herself:

What did I sacrifice in myself just to keep hope alive?

For the one who caused the doubt:

When someone believed in me—did I honor that gift, or manipulate it?

XII. trigger points

you're inconsistent
about everything
but the very things
that hurt me

Reflection:

When someone's actions are unpredictable or evasive, it forces us into a state of constant questioning. We start to wonder whether their words align with their behavior, and whether their intentions are genuine or manipulative. This uncertainty can create an emotional rollercoaster, where one moment we feel close and secure, only to be thrown into confusion the next. The inability to grasp 'what's real' and 'what's not' can destabilize our sense of trust, not just in the person but in our own judgment.

As doubt settles in, we may start questioning our place in the relationship, feeling as though there is no solid foundation to stand on. This emotional unpredictability can stir up insecurities, often bringing past experiences of betrayal or instability to the surface. Consistency is key in establishing trust and recognizing the impact of shiftiness is crucial in regaining clarity and establishing boundaries to protect our emotional health.

Introspect:

In what ways can I protect my emotional well-being when I feel unsure about my partner's intentions?

XIII. rock bottom

how can you hurt me
when i tell you that i love you?
why do you fight me
when it is i that fights for us?
how could it end
when your grip is tight and
won't let me go?
who will it be that tends to you,
when all hope is gone
and you've lost your home?

Reflection:

Love often brings a painful contradiction, where vulnerability meets resistance. Combativeness in love often arises from unresolved conflicts, where instead of working through differences, partners begin to engage in a pattern of defensiveness and confrontation.

This dynamic can stem from unmet needs and a lack of communication, where one or both individuals feel the need to defend themselves rather than seek mutual understanding. Combativeness tends to shift the focus from connection to competition, where winning the argument becomes more important than finding a resolution.

To break free from this cycle, it's essential to prioritize communication, empathy, and self-awareness, creating space for vulnerability rather than defense. When both partners approach the relationship with a willingness to listen and understand, the need for combativeness naturally diminishes. If your partner isn't a willing participant in addressing issues or improving communication, it's important not to blame yourself for their lack. You can only control your own actions and growth, and sometimes, the best you can do is set boundaries and focus on your own healing.

Introspect:

How can I better balance vulnerability and self-protection when I am faced with challenges in my relationship?

XIV. seasons

i can't help but think of warmer days.
a gentle breeze in my ear;
the sun's loving kiss.

but these winter days don't end.
warmth is but a memory,
and i'm far too cold to try...

Reflection:

When unresolved issues pile up and are left unaddressed, they create emotional walls between partners. Instead of engaging openly, we begin to withdraw, choosing silence or indifference over connection. Resentment acts as a barrier, making it harder to express love, vulnerability, and empathy as we become more focused on past hurts than on nurturing the bond. Over time, this emotional distance can lead to feelings of isolation, where both individuals feel disconnected and unloved, even when they are physically close.

We may justify our distance as a form of self-protection or as a response to the other person's behavior, but in doing so, we inadvertently perpetuate the very thing we want to avoid—further disconnection. The longer this distance remains unchallenged, the more ingrained it becomes. Healing from resentment requires honest communication, a willingness to confront underlying issues, and a commitment to rebuilding trust and emotional intimacy with patience and empathy.

Introspect:

How can I resist the temptation to withdraw when faced with challenges in my relationship?

XV. disillusionment

i knew all along
that a different way
was what we both wanted

Reflection:

By the time we reached our eighth wedding anniversary, my husband and I were forced to confront a deeply rooted issue that challenged the very core of our marriage and ourselves: neither of us were happy with the way things were going.

When we deny our own needs, we inadvertently plant seeds of resentment—making it harder to meet our partner's needs, let alone our own. But when we begin to give ourselves the very things we expect from our partner, we show up differently. It is through authenticity that connection and individuality are restored and celebrated.

Introspect:

How can I rekindle my courage and passion to move forward authentically while respecting both my individuality and our marriage?

XVI. hopeless

hopelessness...
the aftermath
of a life never given the chance
to live

Reflection:

Within the sorrow of missed opportunities lies an invitation to reflect and grow. The sense of remorse can become a catalyst for change, urging us to embrace the present moment and the possibilities that still lie ahead. It reminds us that while some chances may have passed, new ones are always unfolding. By acknowledging the pain of the past, we can use it as fuel to live more fully and intentionally, ensuring that the life we have now is given the proper nourishment to thrive.

Introspect:

Which past regrets in your life can you reframe with a more positive outcome?

CHAPTER TWO
OBSCURED

I. unconscious thought

it cost me everything
to make this dream a reality,
not realizing,
it was nightmares
i was manifesting instead.

Reflection:

Unacknowledged or suppressed fears can quietly shape our lives, often leading us down paths we never intended to take. These deep-seated thoughts can manifest in unexpected ways, guided by influences we might not fully recognize. They may show up in patterns of self-sabotage, hesitation, or the avoidance of personal growth. Over time, these hidden fears can limit our potential and keep us trapped in cycles where we've yet to integrate our shadow.

Self-examination allows us to break free from the grip of anxiety and self-doubt, empowering us to take control of our lives. It opens the door to personal growth, as we learn that much of what we fear is often less daunting when confronted directly.

Introspect:

How can I discern and recognize patterns in my behavior that are subtly influenced by unconscious fears?

II. integration

the world splits
his subconscious is
calling to be healed,
restored,
to become anew,
but he fights it,
oh! how he fights!

written somewhere in an ancient script
i recall what it says:

>   *"the way to arrive is in unison"*

but in the light,
i stand alone

Reflection:

The subconscious, like a hidden guide, calls out for healing, for wholeness, and integration. And yet, there's resistance— a fight against the surrender needed for true union. When we allow all parts of ourselves to converge, it is a moment of self-realization and an invitation to reconcile all that divides us— to embrace the understanding that we are not a series of fragmented parts, but a single, resonant whole. Through reflection, we are offered a chance to reconcile that division, allowing all aspects of our being to harmonize. In this wholeness, we are no longer alone but fully present in the journey of becoming.

Introspection:

What am I resisting within myself, and why?

III. repentance

with the eclipse up above me,
the past pulling,
the future calling
i can now see where i'm going.
i walk toward change,
leaving behind
what no longer serves me

Reflection:

Repentance is the process of confronting and acknowledging unconscious behaviors and patterns that have caused harm to ourselves and others. It requires us to face the dissonance between our actions and our deeper values, often revealing hidden fears, unresolved conflicts, or unmet needs that shape our behavior.

When faced with our fears, we often feel like we're navigating a path with no end in sight. Yet, it's within these moments of profound hardship that we can uncover our inner strength. Trusting in something greater than ourselves helps us rise from the depths of our own personal hells. Rather than being about guilt or punishment, repentance is a process of *returning* that requires self-awareness and humility— recognizing the patterns that have led us astray and choosing to heal the wounds beneath them.

Introspect:

In what ways can I embrace my journey through darkness to find healing and renewal?

IV. awareness

i know that one day,
i will give myself love
and spare the pain

Reflection:

The journey of healing uncovers the self-deception we use to justify unkind treatment from others. By acknowledging our excuses, we invite deeper introspection into how we deny our own worthiness of love and acceptance. This process requires confronting the parts of ourselves that have been conditioned to settle for less than we deserve.

Recognizing that self-love is essential for breaking free from these cycles can be both empowering and healing. As we learn to value ourselves, we begin to release the pain of unreciprocated affection and past disappointments.

Introspect:

In what ways can I embrace my own worth and foster self-love to heal from past hurts?

V. your love

a hawk sweeps down,
snatches your offering,
brings it forward
like a sword
cutting all that's not needed away

Reflection:

Dealing with rigid control in a relationship can foster helplessness and disconnection. When one partner exerts excessive control over decisions, emotions, or behaviors, the other often feels undervalued and restricted. This dynamic may stem from the controlling partner's fears or past experiences of hurt. To heal, both partners need to communicate openly and set boundaries that respect autonomy while maintaining connection. Healthy love requires mutual respect, trust, and healthy boundaries.

If you're the controlling partner, this behavior may arise from a desire for security or fear of losing control. Often rooted in past trauma, healing involves self-reflection, confronting insecurities, and learning to trust both the relationship and your partner. Letting go of micromanagement creates space for growth and vulnerability fostering a more balanced and loving connection.

Introspect:

What aspects of your life are you holding onto that may be hindering your capacity to love and receive love fully?

VI. push/pull

you say you want out
yet, you're still here...
reminding me of all the love i could have...
if you'd just transcend or surrender—
or leave, like you say you want to

Reflection:

The push/pull dynamic in a relationship can lead to emotional confusion when one partner alternates between creating distance and seeking closeness when fears of abandonment arise. This pattern often stems from underlying fears of vulnerability or dealing with unresolved shame, causing them to withdraw when the relationship feels too intense, only to reach out again when the distance becomes unsettling.

For the partner on the receiving end, this behavior can feel destabilizing, leaving them uncertain and emotionally strained. For the partner exhibiting the dynamic, it's important to reflect on the fears driving their actions and work towards expressing their needs with honesty and vulnerability. Both partners can benefit from fostering open communication and creating a safe space for trust and understanding, with professional support to help break the cycle.

Introspect:

What is holding me back from either surrendering fully or moving on completely?

VII. not enough/enough

i am the breath,
the beating heart,
holding us together
when
i don't want to go on
without you / can't go on with you

Reflection:

Feeling like you've reached a breaking point in a relationship can be an emotionally complex experience, with years of shared history and deep commitment making it difficult to confront feelings of dissatisfaction or even contemplate change. Recognizing and validating your feelings is the first step toward finding clarity, whether through healing the relationship or exploring a new path.

During these trying times, reconnect with yourself and reflect on what you truly need to feel fulfilled. Honest communication with your partner is essential, provided both are open to listening and working together. Shadow work to compliment therapy—individually or as a couple—can help unpack emotional layers and identify patterns contributing to discontent. Whether the path leads to reconciliation or separation, approach it with compassion for yourself and your partner, acknowledging that growth and change are natural, even after years of shared commitment.

Introspect:

What have I learned about myself through the challenges we've faced together?

VIII. apologies
without change

grace lingers
through apologies without change.
words alone can't heal what's broken

Reflection:

Forgiveness is a generous and powerful act, but when it becomes a one-sided effort, it can feel as though your grace and mercy is being taken for granted. Over time, this dynamic may lead to feelings of resentment, self-doubt, or even hopelessness as repeated forgiveness without results begins to erode trust. It's natural to want to believe in someone's potential to grow, but it's also important to recognize when words are not supported by actions.

True forgiveness doesn't mean enduring cycles of hurt without accountability. It involves setting boundaries and a commitment to self-respect. To heal from this pattern, it's crucial to shift focus inward, asking yourself what you truly need for your emotional well-being. Communicating openly with your partner about how their behavior affects you can provide clarity, but ultimately, if no change occurs, choosing your own growth and peace may be the most compassionate act for both parties. Leaving a relationship should not be the first action taken, but rather a last resort after honest communication, self-reflection, and failed attempts for growth and resolution have been made.

Introspect:

What boundaries can you establish to protect your emotional well-being while offering grace?

IX. acquiescence

why do i cry for the One that causes me pain?
why do i fight
for the One who fights against me, not for me?
why do i stay
when all i/you want to do is leave?

Reflection:

Acquiescing in a relationship often involves going along with your partner's desires, decisions, or behaviors without expressing your own needs or concerns. While this might initially seem like a way to maintain harmony or avoid conflict, it can lead to feelings of resentment, frustration, or emotional disconnection over time. Continually setting aside your voice to prioritize another can erode your sense of self-worth and create an imbalance, where one partner's needs dominate the dynamic while the other feels invisible or unimportant.

Healthy relationships thrive on mutual respect and open communication, where both partners feel valued and heard. If you notice a tendency to acquiesce, it's essential to explore the reasons behind it—whether it stems from a fear of conflict, a need to please, or difficulty asserting yourself. Restoring balance involves setting boundaries, expressing your feelings honestly, and understanding that true connection comes from mutual authenticity, not silent compromise.

Introspect:

In what situations do I find myself acquiescing to my partner? What are the patterns?

X. shattered reflection

it feels like i have been dragging myself
through broken glass
just to feel bad about it

Reflection:

Self-worth is the foundation of how we perceive ourselves and interact with the world. It plays a pivotal role in marriage, yet it can be deeply impacted by childhood trauma. Experiences of neglect, criticism, or inconsistent love during formative years can leave lasting wounds, making it difficult to feel deserving of love. In a marriage, these unresolved feelings may manifest as dependence on a partner for validation. Conflict or perceived rejection can feel overwhelming, reinforcing old insecurities and creating a dynamic where one partner's need for reassurance might inadvertently disrupt the balance of the relationship. Over time, this strain can erode intimacy and trust, making it essential to address the root causes of low self-worth.

Healing self-worth within the context of marriage requires courage and involves recognizing how past experiences influence present interactions. Managing emotions and learning to separate your self-worth from your partner's behaviors are quintessential to your growth and that of your relationship. True self-worth comes from within.

Introspect:

In what ways do you believe your childhood experiences have shaped your expectations in your relationship?

XI. shadow play

oh, how i wish you knew
that you are so much more to me
than just my Shadow.
if only i could convince you
that i'm more than just yours

Reflection:

When our partner embodies our insecurities through their words and actions, it can amplify our struggles with self-acceptance. This dynamic reveals how deeply our relationships can mirror our inner conflicts, making it vital to discern how the behaviors we perceive are projections of our unresolved issues — or a reflection of theirs.

Recognizing this dynamic offers an opportunity for growth and healing as we can choose to address our vulnerabilities and the root of our wounds rather than react defensively. By approaching the situation with a lens of curiosity, we can uncover the lessons these interactions hold, guiding us toward a healthier relationship with ourselves and others.

Introspect:

What hidden aspects of myself might I be projecting onto others? What might be the root of these vulnerabilities?

CHAPTER THREE
ECLIPSED

The months following the summer eclipse of 2024 were among the most challenging of my life. It was the deepest I had ever journeyed, fully aware that I was venturing into the unknown. This awakening sparked the reflections you're reading in this book, guiding me on my path from the depths of the underworld back to the light of life. My old ways of being, existing, and interacting with the world were radically shifting. I had reached new depths of understanding, realizing that I had no choice but to confront the Shadow within —the one holding the keys to the very abyss I found myself in. I understood that the only way out was through.

I. my heart, my shadow

i wish my Shadow would just listen
to my heart
hold it close
and mend it—
let it transform us.

how can it, though,
when it begins in me?

II. realization

i was once sure that i'd be happier without you,
but it crushes me to hear it from you

III. from darkness to light

heartache is felt the most upon waking
when just moments earlier
all was forgotten

IV. prayer

the things i pray for
are sometimes contradictory
when you can't tell
mind and heart apart

V. truth

truth is my reward and
punisher;
a seductive game

VI. breakthrough

oh, to break through!
a shot in the dark,
only to find yourself there

VII. understanding strongholds

how unfortunate for me
to be loved
the way i desire
only after i leave you

VIII. disruption

this silence is
so beautiful.

stay a while...

remember the calm
before you return
to the battlefield
to fight me

IX. finding my voice

in the end,
my projections have
   brought me to face myself,
causing me to find my voice
   in the lifeless dark;
a new tongue that knows its power

X. purification

i release my silence,
purifying the wounds that once kept me captive
now facing a harsher reality
and the sad possibility
of living without you.

i'm finally healing

XI. rising

i held the weight of regret
for far too long;
a stone fixed to my breath
but in stillness,
i let go
to meet myself
at the surface—
a radically new person

LVF LVX

CHAPTER FOUR
AURORAS

The rare beauty of the Auroras is currently unfolding across the globe—a testament to the sun's incredible power. Its brilliant colors spill across our skies during the sun's most active phase gearing towards a rare event known as the solar maximum which occurs every eleven years. This majestic light is a symbol of healing after the storms. From this cosmic fire, a new creation rises in victory, bringing—not just moments of awe and splendor, but also opportunities for spiritual growth.

In the mystical tradition of Kabbalah, the Sephirot—meaning the *spheres of influence* in Hebrew—reveal a path toward self-actualization and sacred union, illuminating divine traits waiting to be embodied as our true selves. In this journey, we see that free will is not merely something to believe in, but a resource waiting to be utilized. By embodying these virtues, we open ourselves to their transformative power, allowing them to influence our thoughts, actions, and relationships.

The healing path, layered with challenges and revelations, teaches us to listen deeply to the soul's wisdom. Even when resistance meets us, or old habits pull us back, we are reminded that all is a choice. Are we ascending or descending? Growing or regressing into toxic patterns?

In that freedom, we awaken the power of will that guides us towards who we are meant to become. Each conscious and intentional decision to embrace life over destruction helps us let go of bitterness, resentment, and anger, bringing forth the opportunity to purify ourselves in the light rather than hide behind empty masks within our darkest shadows.

These poems trace a path of ascension—*The Way to Self*—a journey toward becoming the fullest, truest version of who we are. From self-acceptance to atonement, each step activates the neural and emotional pathways that invite healing into both mind and heart, guiding us back to wholeness and alignment with Source.

I. Malkuth (actualization)

you take me in your arms,
hold me up to the sky—
higher than the sun.

here, the ego sees that
there is something greater than *it,*
now knowing that love is the vessel
which breaks into daylight—
reaching far beyond the veil
where new vows are spoken.

closing the space its shadow created,
we release the division our fear once accepted,
moving from ignorance toward wholeness—
a heavenly foundation
that begins with self-acceptance.

the kingdom awaits

Reflection:

Acceptance and forgiveness are inseparable foundations for personal growth and the unfolding of our highest potential. Together, they mark the essence of Malkuth—the grounding point from which true transformation begins. These intentions mark a pivotal moment of release, freeing us from the weight of past mistakes, regrets, and relational wounds that keep us tethered to old, limiting patterns.

To grow into who we are meant to be, we must first embrace who we are—with all our imperfections. Letting go of guilt and shame creates space for compassion, understanding, and new possibilities to take root. This shift not only fosters healing but also empowers us to step into a more authentic and purposeful version of ourselves. It allows us to rewrite the narrative of our lives, transforming pain into wisdom and obstacles into steppingstones toward our highest potential. In this way, self-forgiveness becomes a radical act of love that radiates outward into every aspect of our existence and allows us to rebuild a strong foundation rooted in truth.

II. Yesod (channel)

a current
awakens the void.
in surrender, i open to receive.
hold my cup up to its voice,
filling in the fragments
of my once broken heart

Reflection:

Yesod plays a vital role in the journey toward actualization, serving as the channel through which emotional and psychological patterns are integrated. It bridges the inner world with outer reality, helping us translate unconscious material into conscious experience.

Through Yesod, we connect with the subconscious mind, where both our deepest wounds and the keys to our healing reside. In the stillness it offers, we learn to listen— uncovering the stories, fears, and beliefs that have shaped us. By working with this energy, we begin to transform old patterns that no longer serve us, making space for wiser, more integrated and healthier ways of being.

III. Hod (surrender)

a man who puts his weapons down
for love
conquers the beast.

he who conquers the beast
conquers my heart

Reflection:

To set aside one's defenses for unity in a relationship is a conscious release of control that invites vulnerability. It is within this act of surrender that true strength arises, soothing the part of us fueled by pride or fear. This inner peace fosters a deeper connection of the heart, revealing the beauty in yielding the ego to a higher power.

The essence of Hod lies in the strength found not in force, but in surrender, inviting us to release our rigid control and trust in the flow of life. It is through surrender that we open ourselves to divine wisdom, allowing our mental structures to soften and our hearts to expand. Through Hod, we learn that surrender is not about giving up but about giving in to a deeper sense of purpose. It is the willingness to acknowledge our limitations and to seek guidance from something greater than ourselves.

In Hod, we find that surrender is not weakness but the truest form of mastery and connection.

IV. Netzach
(victory)

i have done so many things in life, yet not enough.
i felt i had to mold myself into some specific version;
zigzagging
back and forth between the pillars of
Jachin, Boaz.
chasing freedom when I already was
free —
to hideaway,
or live by the sword.

no, no, no...
see, i had it all wrong.
i realize that now
having forgotten my name.
despite my growing older,
wiser,
closer than i've ever been —
it cost me beauty for beauty,
and pain for pain.
if only
i had known,
it was me i was after.

Reflection:

In *Netzach*, healing unfolds when we realize that we are inseparable from our shadows—and that true victory comes not from avoiding pain, but from confronting it. As we engage with these hidden aspects of ourselves, we discover they carry invaluable lessons, often guiding us toward growth and self-discovery. Rather than viewing them as separate, we begin to recognize our shadows as integral to our wholeness.

Shadow integration reveals the roles we've played in our own suffering, enabling us to release old patterns and step into a new chapter with strength, wisdom, and grace. Ultimately, we come to understand that our greatest victories don't arise from the absence of struggle, but from the courage to face our fears head-on.

Transforming them into catalysts for profound personal evolution is the victory our souls require.

V. Tifaret
(optimism)

look for the beauty in all things—
in the cracks of your heart
in the stillness between breaths
in hallow longings of night
and you will find your Self there
with open arms

Reflection:

In the wisdom of Tiphareth, beauty is revealed not just in moments of ease, but in the alchemy of our trials, where each hardship becomes a steppingstone toward wholeness. These challenges can serve as profound teachers that shape our character, illuminating strengths and resilience we never knew we had.

By seeking beauty in our darkest moments, we transform our perspective, turning pain into wisdom and sorrow into growth. This journey calls us to embrace life's complexities, where beauty and resilience intertwine to shape our path forward. In recognizing the profound lessons hidden within hardship, we discover a deeper connection to ourselves and to life itself. It is through embracing this beauty that we align with our true self, finding the divine in both the perfect and the imperfect, and reclaiming our power to create meaning from every experience.

VI. Gevurah
(strength)

strength is the spirit that doesn't break
amid releasing the darkness
you once couldn't see

Reflection:

Gevurah, the energy of strength and discipline, manifests in our ability to confront the shadow. This process is not without its struggle, but it is within this challenge that true power is revealed. It is the strength required to release what no longer serves us, even when it feels overwhelming or frightening. To face the shadow is to confront our deepest fears, wounds, and vulnerabilities, and to acknowledge the parts of us that we have long ignored or denied. Releasing the shadow is not a momentary act; it is a continuous process that requires patience, perseverance, and self-compassion.

This empowering force encourages us to embrace the struggle, knowing that on the other side lies freedom, clarity, and the opportunity for renewal. The shadow, once integrated, makes way for a deeper understanding of who we are and who we are becoming.

VII. Chesed
(grace)

the pitch of an instrument, finely tuned.
a love, boundless and pure.
a loving smile when all is said and done

Reflection:

Amid life's challenges, there is often a hidden grace that unfolds when we allow ourselves to be vulnerable, embracing the imperfections that define our human experience. Extending grace to ourselves means forgiving our missteps and allowing room for growth without judgment. By offering this same grace to others, we create an environment where healing is possible, and connection becomes a natural, restorative force.

As we embody the influence of Chesed, we begin to see its reflection in our interactions, nurturing a sense of altruism in our shared humanity. It is in this space that we learn to love more freely, to listen more deeply, and to move more gracefully in the world.

VIII. Binah (understanding)

in wholeness—
we see anew
all that we once denied.
a thread unwound.

to be understood—
the greatest pleasure of all.

and to understand—
the greatest gift

Reflection:

In Binah, understanding emerges as a profound catalyst for transformation, inviting us to delve deep into the complexities of our experiences and the lives of others. It requires a willingness to listen—truly listen—beyond the surface, to grasp the emotions and stories that shape our realities. As we do so, we open ourselves to the divine wisdom flowing through every moment, guiding us toward greater clarity and compassion.

Through understanding, we cultivate a deeper awareness of ourselves and our surroundings. It allows us to see challenges not as insurmountable obstacles, but as opportunities for empathy, where we discover the beauty of connection, illuminating paths previously shrouded in darkness.

IX. Chokmah (wisdom)

yielding to the unseen,
        and
guided by a light that
no shadow can devour—
lies a bridge where
the heart meets
eternity

Reflection:

In Chokmah, wisdom is the deep and intuitive understanding that arises from lived experience, reflection, and discernment. It is the ability to see beyond immediate appearances, connecting actions and choices to their broader, often unseen, consequences. Wisdom integrates knowledge with compassion, guiding one toward what is just, true, and life-affirming. It is the art of aligning one's thoughts, words, and deeds with a higher sense of purpose.

Wisdom listens before speaking, seeks to heal rather than harm, and values the balance between what is known and the humility of what remains unknown. Chokmah teaches us to recognize the interconnectedness of all beings, encouraging us to cultivate a deeper appreciation for the journey itself.

X. Keter
(crown)

to walk the jagged line,
we turn away from darkness,
letting go of what we once were.
to become new, we lay bare the hidden,
and in that surrender,
we find freedom.

for it is in this space
that we rise, like gods,
knowing both good and evil—
choosing holiness, as near as we can grasp,
to transcend the ether.

Reflection:

The essence of healing asks us to face ourselves fully, bringing what's hidden into light. Within the essence of Kether, atonement becomes possible, inviting us to reconcile with ourselves. It's in that release that we meet the divine within.

Atonement is one of quiet transformation, calling us to confront our actions, our words, and even our silences. It requires us to see ourselves honestly, to acknowledge the places where we've caused pain or let bitterness take root. This path is not an easy one; it's lined with the echoes of choices we might rather forget. Yet, in facing these moments directly, we create a way forward, stepping out of the shadows of regret and into a state of self-realization.

It is through this awareness that we can shed old identities that no longer fit, leaving behind the burdens of pride or fear. It's an act of surrender, not to another's will, but to the truth within us guided by divinity itself. As we offer release—to ourselves and to others—we dissolve the ties that keep us bound to the past. This is the path of becoming. In this journey, we awaken to a more profound understanding, bridging the chasm between who we have been and who we are becoming. We begin to align with this vision through the embodiment of these life-changing attributes, bringing us into self-actualization and finally, union with Source.

Alas, the crown of life.

LVF LVX

EPILOGUE

Most of us live in a perpetual state of unawareness; a quiet dormancy where truth hides in the shadows. The journey inwards into our shadow realm is both fierce and necessary. Descending into our own underworld, we confront the dark truths and lost fragments buried within, facing the pain we once avoided and the fears we long kept away.

These shadows serve to remind us of the duality inherent in all growth: light and dark, bliss and suffering, expansion and contraction. In these depths, there are no false pretenses, no illusions. We are stripped bare, forced to see ourselves clearly and feel the weight of truth. And yet, in this struggle, we begin to find strength, peeling away layers that no longer serve our path to healing.

Emerging from the depths, we step gradually into the light where we begin to integrate both the light and dark, acknowledging the necessity of each in our journey. The more we ascend, the more we embody the Sephirot— the sacred pathways of divine traits that illuminate our path.

Rooted in this wisdom, we move beyond mere survival into a state of grace and equilibrium. Each sphere of the Sephirot becomes a compass, guiding us toward balance and harmony. We realize that healing is not a single endpoint but a continuous, spiraling evolution, one that can restore our wholeness and repair relationships with those closest to us. We become alchemists, merging light and shadow, transmuting pain into wisdom and fear into love.

Each step forward, no matter how small, is a victory over the shadows that once bound us. By integrating our shadow, we claim the fullness of who we are and step into a future shaped by intention and grace. This is the gift of healing— not just for ourselves, but for generations to come—as we break cycles, mend wounds, and plant seeds of hope.

As we continue to rise, we transcend our inner world through compassion and grace, creating a ripple that touches all we encounter. In this union of mind, heart, and spirit, we come closer to the divine, embodying our deepest purpose: to reflect a light that endures beyond time, transforming ourselves and the world around us.

May you walk forward with courage, knowing that even in your darkest moments, you hold the power to love.

GLOSSARY

adaptive child
the part of the psyche developed in childhood to manage pain or unmet needs. this version of the self is often reactive, defensive, or controlling in adulthood.

alchemize
to transform, especially in a spiritual or emotional sense—turning pain into wisdom.

ascension
a process of spiritual elevation or enlightenment; rising in consciousness.

ascension
a process of spiritual elevation or enlightenment that recognizes ego traps; rising in consciousness.

ascension path
a spiritual journey toward higher consciousness through personal growth and shadow work.

atonement
a return to wholeness through reconciliation with the self, others, and Source.

Binah (understanding)
insight; the ability to process wisdom with compassion.

Carl Jung
Swiss psychiatrist who founded analytical psychology. known for concepts like the shadow, archetypes, individuation, and the collective unconscious.

channel
a conduit for spiritual energy or divine insight; often the bridge between inner and outer worlds.

Chesed (grace)
mercy and loving-kindness; divine generosity and compassion.

Chokmah (wisdom)
intuitive knowing and divine inspiration; the seed of all intellectual and spiritual creation.

collective unconscious
Jung's concept of a shared unconscious containing universal archetypes and instincts.

dissociation
a psychological defense mechanism involving detachment from reality or the self, often due to trauma.

duality
the coexistence of opposing forces (e.g., light/dark, ego/soul) that are interdependent and often reconciled in inner work.

ego
the conscious self; the mediator between the inner world and external reality, shaping identity.

generational trauma
emotional wounds and behavioral patterns passed down through families, often unconsciously.

Gevurah (strength)
judgment and discipline; the capacity to set boundaries and uphold truth.

Hod (surrender)
in kabbalah, symbolizes humility and the release of control; inner peace through yielding.

id

the primitive, instinctual part of the psyche driven by the pleasure principle.

individuation

the Jungian process of becoming one's true self by integrating the conscious and unconscious.

inner child

the childlike part of the psyche shaped by early experiences; often in need of healing.

integration

bringing unconscious aspects of the self into conscious awareness for wholeness and healing.

Jachin & Boaz

the symbolic pillars of Solomon's temple representing polarity and the soul's spiritual journey.

Keter (crown)

the highest Sefirah on the Tree of Life, representing the divine origin of will and consciousness; the highest point of spiritual unity with Source.

Machiavellian traits
 manipulative and deceitful behaviors marked by self-interest and a lack of ethical concern.

Malkuth (actualization)
 the physical world— where embodiment, manifestation, and reality take root.

Netzach (victory)
 persistence and triumph through self-awareness; enduring challenge with strength.

neural pathways
 networks in the brain that influence how we think, act, and process experiences.

neuroplasticity
 the brain's ability to form new neural connections through learning and healing.

persona
 the mask or identity one presents to the world to meet social expectations, distinct from the true self.

projection
 attributing one's own unconscious feelings or thoughts onto someone else.

psychic imprint
 emotional or energetic residue from past experiences
that unconsciously shape perception and behavior.

psycho-spiritual
 relating to the integration of psychological and
spiritual growth and insight.

psycho-spiritual journey
 a path of inner evolution integrating both
psychological insight and spiritual awareness.

purification
 a symbolic or spiritual cleansing of the psyche or
soul; shedding what no longer serves.

Qliphoth
 in Kabbalah, the shadow realms representing
imbalance, corruption, and separation from Source; a
distortion of the Sephirot; akin to the *Tree of Good &*
Evil

sacred union
 inner wholeness achieved through balancing the
feminine and masculine, or the ego and soul.

self-actualization
the realization and embodiment of one's fullest
potential and higher self.

self-awareness
conscious understanding of one's own character,
motives, and emotions.

self-discovery
the process of uncovering one's authentic identity,
desires, and values.

self-forgiveness
releasing guilt and shame to accept one's humanity
and move forward with compassion.

self-inquiry
the practice of asking deep, reflective questions to
understand one's true nature.

self-realization
awakening to one's true self beyond ego; inner clarity
and alignment with purpose.

Sephirot
the ten divine emanations in Kabbalah that reflect
aspects of consciousness and creation. together, they

form the path to sacred union with the Self and the Divine, akin to *The Tree of Life*.

shadow
 the unconscious aspects of the psyche, often repressed or hidden, containing both wounds and wisdom.

solar maximum
 the sun's peak activity cycle, symbolizing personal intensity and transformation.

strongholds
 persistent patterns or beliefs rooted in fear or trauma that hinder growth.

subconscious
 the part of the mind below conscious awareness, storing memories, emotions, and instincts.

superego
 the moral conscience shaped by societal and parental values; counterbalances the id.

survival instincts
 instinctive responses to danger or stress—fight, flight, freeze, or fawn.

Tifaret (optimism)
balance and compassion; the spiritual heart, and the center of gravity in the Sephirotic structure — a place where opposites are reconciled.

transformation
a profound inner shift that leads to healing, clarity, and empowerment.

transmutation
the spiritual or emotional process of transforming pain, fear, or shadow into wisdom and growth.

trigger
an emotional reaction caused by unresolved past experiences or trauma cues.

Yesod (channel)
the foundation and filter between the subconscious and the external world; integration point.

LVF LVX

ABOUT THE AUTHOR

LVF is a writer, mystic, and shadow work coach whose work blends personal insight, psychoanalysis, and ethereal wisdom helping to guide individuals toward healing. Drawing from first-hand experiences, her work illuminates the path toward growth and transformation. With a background in philosophy and a master's degree in conflict resolution, she invites readers to embark on a journey of self-actualization through shadow work.

@LVF.SHADOWWORK | LVFLVX.COM

LVF LVX